the last
ROCK

there's a cure for addictions

ROGER FORMIGONI

the last
ROCK

there's a cure for addictions

Preface by
EDIR MACEDO

1st Edition
Rio de Janeiro
2014

Unipro
EDITORA

GENERAL COORDINATION
Renato Cardoso

GENERAL DIRECTOR
Paulo Lopes

EXECUTIVE PUBLISHER
Vera Léa Camelo

GRAPHIC DESIGNER
Rafael Nicolaevsky Pinheiro

ARTWORK
Rafael Brum

TYPESETTING
Rosemeri Melgaço, Luis Bernardino, Sandra Gouvêa and Curso ER

ENGLISH VERSION
David Higginbotham and Sandra Gouvêa

PICTURES OF THE COUPLE
Demetrio Koch Jr.

1st edition | 1st print

F723l Formigoni, Roger
      The Last Rock: There's a cure for addictions
      Unipro Publisher, Rio de Janeiro, August 2014. 1st edition
      112 pp.: il.: 21 cm

      ISBN **978-85-7140-717-6**

      1. Addictions.   2. Freedom from drugs.   3. Change of life.
      I. Title

                                           CDD 243

UNIPRO EDITORA
ESTRADA ADHEMAR BEBIANO, 3.610 – INHAÚMA
CEP 20766-720 – RIO DE JANEIRO – RJ
TEL.: (21) 3296-9393
WWW.UNIPRO.COM.BR

C O N T E N T

P R E F A C E

Edir Macedo

The only way to permanently solve the suffering of people — and in particular those lost in the endless maze of pain we call drug addiction — is faith in God. At times people in this trap seek solace in prayer, in a word, a message, a beautiful song... but none of these will ever solve the deep-seated problem that afflicts them.

They need more than mere comfort. What piece of advice has the power to help people lost in this world of pain and alienation? What can help people who are cut off from everyone they love, and who are being attacked by a deadly urge that overshadows everything that is truly important in their lives?

Who, other than God Himself, can deliverance these people? His only desire for suffering people is that they get free... that they are saved from the ruthless disease of drug addiction, a plague that has forced its way into their lives.

Many argue that suffering is part of the process of purification, that it is karma, or that it is the cross we have to carry, a trial from God that we should simply accept. Others even say that the pain of suffering people is fate...

Spending rivers of money on the problem is something that has often been proved a waste. Even experts in the field admit that they do not see positive results in any case. In fact, some refer their patients to the Universal Church because its success rate is so high.

Whatever the addiction, it's important to understand that there is a spirit behind it all, a negative force that takes a hold of the nervous system of an addict and controls him. The same nervous system that compels us to do good, can lead us to do evil.

The spirit of addiction is responsible for an addict's behavior. It is an evil spirit whose role is to control the addict, and because of this, any treatment that fails to attack this spirit will be utterly ineffective. It can only be removed by the power of faith.

Because of this, anyone with a drug addiction should pay no attention to clichés and superficial advice. They should look to the Word of God that tells us that, no matter the situation, faith has the power to solve it.

Faith is a fountain of life and solutions... of answers from God. Faith is life — addiction leads to death. When it comes to people lost in the endless maze of drugs, having faith in the Word and allowing Jesus to manifest in their lives is the only way to truly fight and defeat their problem.

May God bless you all in Jesus' name.

CHAPTER I

I am Roger Formigoni, an ordinary guy just like you who've chosen to read this book. Because I too am made of flesh and blood, I was tempted by the things of this world and unfortunately gave in. As a result, I wasted seven years of my life in the addictions of illegal drugs and sexual immorality. I was a hostage for all this time, a prisoner of drugs, and witnessed the horrors that people who are lost in this kind of life face every day, and of which many say there is no way out.

All my choices were made of my own free will. I am going to tell you my story in the following pages, a story of how I stepped into this unthinkable world of drugs. You will also hear the thoughts of those who lived with me at the time. All these people played important roles by my side, witnessing all my worst moments. It was a tough period of time when I repeatedly made bad decisions. These eye-witness testimonies are spread throughout the book, and give a good idea of who I was.

> *"I got to the point that one night
> I smoked over one hundred rocks
> of crack. I bought cocaine and marijuana
> by the kilo to use in endless wild parties."*
> **Roger Formigoni**

It was a risk few people would take. I would snort an entire plate of cocaine by myself, or a line of cocaine one meter long. At one point I was out of control and would throw everything and everyone together — any available drugs and anyone I happened to cross paths with. In the following pages, you will understand, step by step, how I stooped to this.

Though my choices put me on a chaotic path, my childhood was normal. I played with friends and enjoyed sports. I was the tallest in my class so I was a natural for basketball and volleyball. Our home was very quiet, with no major problems. My parents were pleasant, were always there for us, and disciplined their children when necessary... my sisters and me. There was nothing that could have led me to addictions, except for my own choices. Life presents us with all kinds of opportunities, some good, some not so good.

I lived in Lucélia, a city in the countryside of the state of São Paulo. It was the late 1980s. I started working at an early age, a carpentry apprentice at a vocational school at the age of 12. It wasn't exactly a job; I was being trained. And that's where I began to experience drugs. The strong smell of shoe glue was the first item on my menu of illegal drugs.

Shoe glue

Abusers of inhalants breathe them in through the nose or mouth in a variety of ways (known as "huffing"). Although the high produced by inhalants usually lasts just a few minutes, abusers often try to prolong it by continuing to inhale repeatedly over several hours.

SIDE EFFECTS: dizziness, nausea, sneezing, coughing, salivation and photophobia (extreme sensitivity to light).

ADAPTED FROM

I sniffed so much glue that one day I had an accident that could have been very serious, given the circumstances. One afternoon, after sniffing glue all day long, I climbed to the top of a wall. (I do not remember why.) I was so high on the drug that I fell off, flat on my face and broke my nose. This was my first negative experience with drugs. It was the only thing I could get my hands on at the time, but the spiritual damages were already well advanced.

From carpentry school I went to my first real job, at 13, a fiberglass swimming pool factory. Already

Fotolia

addicted to sniffing glue, I developed new addictions that lasted to the age of 19. In the seven years of addiction that followed, I left inhalants for cigarettes, progressed to marijuana, cocaine, experimented with hallucinogenic teas (mostly mushroom), and used ecstasy and LSD, and amphetamine-alcoholic beverages (usually whiskey), I took prescription medication — controlled drugs ("co-pilots") and finally arrived at crack, the rock of death.

Amphetamines

Stimulants temporarily increase alertness and energy. One of the commonly used street drugs that falls into this category are amphetamines (speed, uppers, truck drivers). Prescription stimulants come in tablets or capsules and are swallowed, injected in liquid form or crushed and snorted. The exhaustion that follows leads the stimulant user to want more.

Fotolia

I was already on a path of drug use. I was now using the stronger inhalants that I came in contact with at the swimming pool factory where I worked. I was between 13 and 14 at the time. Even my manager smoked marijuana on the job. My many mistakes were based on the typical, irresponsible curiosity of a teenager, and chronic misinformation. All this turned my life into a tangled maze.

My yearning to be an "adult" drove me to make bad decisions at a stage in my life when my character was being formed.

I worked at that company for years and learned to do my job well. Sadly, the place that opened the door to an honest job ended up being a school for my first addiction. Though I was young, I knew a lot of people, many of whom I have had the pleasure of meeting again, after beating my addictions. I'll talk more about that later.

Drugs became more and more a part of my daily life. At the swimming pool factory, I came across several substances that gave me a rush — a brief altered state of consciousness. The main one was paint thinner.

Besides paint thinner, there was acetone, resins and ether, which I also abused. All of them gave a sense of euphoria when I huffed them. "Poppers" and "whippets" were

Inhalants

More than 1,000 household and other common products could be abused as inhalants: glue, toluene, gasoline, lighter fluid, nitrous oxide, spray paint, correction fluid, cleaning fluid, amyl nitrite, and lacquer thinner or other paint solvents.

SIDE EFFECTS: serious and sometimes irreversible damage to the brain, irregular and rapid heart beat, rashes around nose and mouth, nausea, nosebleeds, muscle fatigue.

ADAPTED FROM

popular versions at concerts and nightclubs. These substances opened the door to something very evil. My co-workers and I would huff anything and everything, looking for a high, a "kick" from the poor man's pot.

The truth is I wasn't interested in the high itself as much as I wanted attention, knowing full well that this was the wrong way to be popular. At school and in my neighborhood I began to hang out with new upper middle class "friends." My knowledge of drugs got me into their group. I eventually became a type of Heisenberg long before Breaking Bad aired on TV.

Contact with these new friends threw open the doors of addiction for me. While I huffed thinner and other chemicals at the factory, and made them available to the employees there, I developed more addictions. I taught them and they taught me. One was tobacco.

CHAPTER II

The first time I inhaled a cigarette I did it for laughs. I remember that with a lot of regret today. To me smokers seemed to be the ones that excelled in their classes, to be respected and mature. And I wanted to be one of them.

Now I know I was not alone in this. Facts clearly show that the world is increasingly turning to drugs. A 2013 report on drug use by the United Nations (World Drug Report) stated, "the cocaine market appears to be expanding in South America and emerging economies in Asia." Cocaine production, for example, "ranged from 776 to 1051 tons in 2011," and "the world's largest cocaine seizures... continue to occur in Colombia (200 tons) and the USA (94 tons)."

The report continues by stating, "Seizures of crystal meth-amphetamine, however, increased to 8.8 tons, the highest level in the last five years, indicating that the substance is an imminent threat." Finally, the report also shows that cannabis remains the most widely used illicit substance "with 180 million consumers, or 3.9 percent of the world population aged 15-64." I was definitely not alone in the world.

Tobacco and nicotine

Cigarette smoke contains over 4,700 chemical compounds including 60 known carcinogens. There is conclusive evidence to indicate that long-term (years) smoking greatly increases the likelihood of developing numerous fatal conditions.

<u>SIDE EFFECTS:</u> anxiety, depression, drowsiness or difficulty in sleeping and occurrence of nightmares; headaches, concentration problems; chronic obstructive pulmonary disease and various cancers.

ADAPTED FROM

For a while I thought I was safe. The inhalants seemed harmless and tobacco (nicotine) was legal. At the time, I never imagined that smoking a couple cigarettes would create an addiction. All teenagers have an exaggerated sense of self-confidence, and yet do not know themselves well enough to exert the proper self-control.

Fotolia

From that cigarette, other thoughts emerged. I really thought that ground up tobacco leaves rolled up in a piece of paper was a symbol of my greatness, the banner of my amazing future – I only needed to master the habit and smoke only when I chose to. But nicotine is unforgiving. According to the World Health Organization, nicotine reaches a person's brain in less than ten seconds and is as addictive as heroin. For the large majority of smokers it becomes a habit. Less than ten percent can quit the habit for longer than one month.

But looking cool was fundamental to my little world. The cigarette that I had tried for laughs gave me a sense of self-worth among my new upper-middle-class girls and friends. Obviously, I had a serious problem of low self-esteem. I desperately needed to be accepted by a group, and would do anything to make friends and overcome my poor social skills. I wouldn't have blamed people for imagining that I had no loving home, or that I was an orphan.

But that had never been true. In contrast to what some may think my parents were always there for me, as I have already mentioned. They always encouraged me to stay away from bad friends and drugs. They did all they could to guide me in life, but I chose to go the other way (with the help of my "friends"). The choice was all mine. A choice which led to more choices, to a never ending game of increasingly significant and cruel challenges, involving a prize that never satisfied, but which always seemed worth it. Pure and utter illusion.

This life of bad choices got pretty rough. I went through hard times as a teenager. I got into a lot of fights at school. But though I had become an angry, aggressive boy, I refused to take my abusive attitude home with me. I thought I was a man because I smoked and got high. I thought I was better than other people and just wanted to live in the moment, ignoring the consequences. I assumed there would be no negative consequences.

Up to that time, those initial addictions fed my ego, and that was enough for me. It's as if the chemicals and nicotine I inhaled convinced me that my life would be an endless series of personal victories. What I did not know, and did not care to know as a young man that got angry at anyone who tried to tell him anything, was that the cigarettes I was smoking had the potential to cause any number of fifty different diseases in my body — heart and circulation problems, as well as cancers and respiratory diseases.

If someone had come up to me with sound medical proof that each time I inhaled I was breathing in 4,700 different toxic substances, I would have laughed in his face. Unknowingly I was allowing tobacco to rule over my brain.

CHAPTER III

Chemical inhalants and nicotine had already become established day-to-day habits. It was a way to assert myself, to be the most "popular" guy among my classmates. But these substances were not the only doorway into the world of addictions. By then, the appeal of cigarettes and inhalants had worn off in terms of physical sensation. Then marijuana made its appearance.

When "friends" introduced me to herb or Mary J, they told me I would experience a trip to another world when I smoked my first spliff. The problem was, no one told me it would be a one-way trip.

Marijuana

Marijuana is the word used to describe the dried flowers, seeds and leaves of the Indian hemp plant. This drug is a hallucinogen. The chemical in cannabis that creates this distortion is known as "THC."

<u>SIDE EFFECTS:</u> intoxication, dry mouth, accelerated heart rate, difficulty coordinating movement and balance, and slow reactions and reflexes. The cardiac rate of people with high blood pressure has been known to double in some cases.

ADAPTED FROM

Fotolia

> "Chaos calls to chaos, to the tune of whitewater rapids. Your breaking surf, your thundering breakers crash and crush me."
>
> **Psalm 42:7 (MSG)**

Chaos calls for more chaos, and not long after I immersed myself in marijuana, other drugs came along — "the cocktail." I led a double life. At home I was one person, on the street I was a completely different person. It was like the novel "The Strange Case of Dr Jekyll and Mr Hyde," by nineteenth century Scottish author Robert Louis Stevenson. My habits had changed. I would come home late, at four or five in the morning, and then go to work at the normal time a few hours later, God knows in what condition.

I was in the phase of trying anything that would give me a high, that would give me hallucinations or feelings of euphoria, wellbeing or inspiration. The sensations would vary, but the significance of my experiences were much more profound. There was a sense of power to which I continually surrendered.

Marijuana was definitely different from inhalants and cigarettes. THC, the active ingredient in marijuana, gave me an extreme sense of relaxation, and so I felt calm and reassured. When I smoked it, I traveled to a world of illusion and no longer worried about anything.

THC (with the molecular formula of $C_{21}H_{30}O_2$) is also found in hemp, and acts directly on the central nervous system of an addict causing numbness, and a decrease in psychomotor and muscle performance, while the user has a sense of well-being, euphoria, drowsiness and hypoglycemia. This sense of "well-being" cost me dearly...

I was destroying the confidence that my parents had place in me. I was tormented by the thought that I might hurt my parents, and so I did everything I could to avoid any suspicion at home. But the physical changes in me were visible. My eyes were constantly bloodshot because of marijuana, so I used eye drops to mask my condition.

The mixture of substances that I used (paint thinner, cigarettes, acetone and other substances like the resin used in the manufacture of pools) gave me the kick I was after. But this same kick had a rebound effect on my schoolwork. I passed that year by cheating off my schoolmates.

After high school, I passed the university entrance exam for accounting, which I attended only up to the fourth semester (the second year of the course). I didn't fail any subject, but I kept everything rolling on the basis of cheat sheets. I learned nothing. I passed subjects by cheating on exams because I wanted my parents to think I was following their advice. I just didn't understand at the time that their advice did not include the farce I was playing.

What was important to me was my group of cool friends. They called me Big Rodge because of my high tolerance for drugs. My best friend was Luciano, who everyone called Lu F[1] (Luciano Farinha). I also had the

---

[1]Luciano Ricardo Marques, my friend in Lucélia, also known as Lu F, or Luciano Farinha.

inside track on upper-middle-class girls. Emboldened by drugs, I could approach these beautiful and liberated girls. Their attitudes had an effect on me; they made me feel good.

> "We used a lot of drugs together. Marijuana, cocaine, mushroom tea, ether spray. We had binges in motels and at my father's small farmhouse. We would buy kilos of pure cocaine to snort, would measure out lines of the stuff with a measuring tape and Big Rodge would snort more than a meter."
>
> *Lu F*

Today I know this was all a false sense of security — a mask that helped me to appear to be the strong man I thought I was, when in truth there was a very weak person behind it all. The availability of drugs and the encouragement of friends turned my addiction into my master. What seemed like pleasure became a suffocating mire.

Prostitutes and every type of alcohol gave a finishing touch to this picture of human degradation. Of course, back then I didn't stop to question what marijuana was, where it came from, its composition or effects. I just wanted to feel the lift. I wasn't interested in details.

> *"We were like zombies — partying all the time, often with women, crashing at my uncle's motels, taking road trips. We had lots of call girls, but other girls too, that would use drugs with us."*
>
> *Lu F*

What I thought would be a temporary experiment became a routine. Smoking spliffs had become a part of my life. Every day I would immerse myself in the world of parties, prostitution, orgies and other disgusting things that I have a hard time writing or speaking about, and that I only talk about as part of my testimony.

I don't know how long it took me to go from one level to the next in this cocktail of addictions. First came cigarettes and inhalants, then came marijuana. What would be next?

CHAPTER IV

In the midst of this degradation, the time came for me to snort, or pop, my first line of cocaine... thanks to the friends I hung around with. A line is the same thing as a bump or a rail of cocaine — a certain amount of powder arranged in a line to be inhaled.

Cocaine

The word cocaine refers to the drug in a powder form or crystal form. Extracted from coca leaves, cocaine was originally developed as a painkiller. It is most often sniffed, with the powder absorbed into the bloodstream through the nasal tissues. It can also be ingested or rubbed into the gums.

<u>SIDE EFFECTS:</u> loss of appetite, increased heart rate, muscular spasms and convulsions, severe depression, paranoia, uncontrolled drug addiction and suicidal tendencies.

ADAPTED FROM

Cocaine was very different than marijuana. It was a power-high. My reflexes increased, and I felt stronger... Above all there was the euphoria. I felt smart and awake, and was overcome by a courage that I would never have had without it.

> "Big Rodge and I practically lived on cocaine. When we were in Lucélia, the devil trembled. It was one party after another. One time Big Rodge, crazy as he was, pulled out a .38 and started shooting at the coconuts in the backyard of the house we were in. The problem was, it was three in the morning! Even worse, he didn't even hit one. People came to Rodge because he knew how to cut cocaine."[2]
>
> *Lu F*

---

[2] The procedure of making pure cocaine powder stretch by mixing it with other substances. It is normally mixed with talc, baking powder, powdered aspirin, flour, sugar, etc.. These impurities represent between 30 to 70% of the final weight of cocaine.

I began to sniff every day, but continued my addiction of inhalants, cigarettes and marijuana, and just mixing everything together. During that time, I would use several bags a day. (Today, cocaine in Brazil is sold in "pinos," small plastic containers.) But when the effects wore off, grief, sadness, depression, and emptiness came rushing in — even thoughts of killing myself passed through my head.

" P i n o "

A common type of consumer packaging for cocaine in Brazil. It is a small plastic capsule that usually contains at least 1g of the drug.

I spent my entire salary to maintain my addiction. My family never asked for a penny at home, and so what I earned would last only one day and go down the drain of drugs. I was falling into a dark hole that was getting deeper each and every moment. Sadly, I was blind to this reality. I lived in the illusion that everything was wonderful. There was no shortage of parties, there were women of all types and ages, and there were prostitutes. That was my life when it was ruled by the cruelty of drugs.

> *"Our bond was cocaine. I remember the day Big Rodge almost got arrested. He had a red motorcycle... We were on our way to a gym in Lucélia to use drugs. He led the way, with a large amount of drugs. When I arrived, the place was packed with police and everyone was being searched... That day he was so close to being arrested."*
>
> *Lu F*

In front of my parents and family I acted like a saint. But as soon as I would go out, the honest truth is that I would experience a personality change. There was a phase when I was out of control. I snorted too much cocaine and smoked too much marijuana. No one I knew was able to keep up with me when it came to using drugs.

> *"We drove like a couple of crazy people. We were traveling at 200 km an hour (125 mph), snorting lines from a plate of cocaine, steering the car with our knees... Life was one big party. Our only thought was drugs. We would go on one, two, three-day drug binges."*
>
> *Lu F*

Where was I going to end up? I wasn't looking for answers. I just wanted drugs, and more drugs. Still not satisfied, I got more inhalants (glue, ether and benzene), added amphetamines that I sometimes mixed with whiskey, psychedelic mushrooms, LSD and ecstasy. This was my drug cocktail version 2.0.

> *"Our noses bled; they were destroyed.*
> *I think it was the acid.*
> *Our noses were completely seared inside.*
> *We snorted cocaine by the meter*
> *at the farmhouse."*
>
> *Lu F*

Of all these drugs, what frightened me the most was psychedelic mushroom tea. I had a hallucinogenic experience with some friends of mine that scared me so much that I actually reconsidered the path I was on. It happened like this. One day I went out to pick mushrooms. Kids in Brazil call this mushroom "frog's house" and they grow in fields of grass. They look like Smurf cartoon mushrooms.

Psychedelic mushrooms

The number of fungi containing psilocybin and psilocin (the active substance) exceeds 50 species. The effects range from mild feelings of relaxation, giddiness, euphoria, visual enhancement (seeing colors brighter), visual disturbances (moving surfaces, waves), to delusions, altered perception of real events, images and faces, or real hallucinations.

<u>SIDE EFFECTS:</u> nausea, muscular weakness, changes in perception and reasoning that can last from three to eight hours.

ADAPTED FROM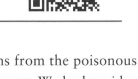

We separated the good mushrooms from the poisonous ones, and ended up with a huge amount. We had no idea how to use them. Again, we were victims of curiosity and misinformation.

We made mushroom tea and drank it as we talked. Sitting on a bench in the neighborhood square, opposite the railway station, we waited for the effects to kick in while we smoked marijuana. Thirty minutes passed and nothing. All of a sudden we exchanged glances and burst into uncontrollable laughter. There were seven of us, all teenagers. Soon we were all crying.

Then came the hallucinations. The world around us became vibrant — green was REALLY green, and blue was REALLY blue... Everything we saw seemed to be in HD. We got up and went over to walk on the train tracks, still laughing. If a train had come along at that moment, it would have run us over and we wouldn't have even cared.

We had frightening hallucinations. The walls of houses seemed to be melting. I felt as if the ground was made of glass and I could see things crawling beneath its surface. Solid objects changed their shape, moved, and seemed to be alive. I was 14 or 15 at the time. We just kept walking. We had no idea of time or space, and ended up outside the city limits of our small town.

Then we started to feel a great deal of paranoia. We confused a factory whistle for police sirens, imagining that we were being chased. We ended up hiding for over an hour, afraid of being arrested. The effect of the drug combination seemed like it would never wear off.

> *"We were constantly running from the police. We sniffed cocaine endlessly and felt like we were going to die. We had taken LSD and mushroom tea. I don't even remember anymore how many times I thought I was at the point of death. After hanging around the public square near Dani's bar, Big Rodge and I walked over to the hospital where the building columns seemed to be melting..."*
>
> *Lu F*

Time passed. We came out of hiding and began to walk with no idea of where we were or where we were going. Our own distress frightened the people we passed by, but the most terrifying aspect was that, as much as we tried, we could not end the trance we were in. For more than eight hours we were trapped under the influence of that drug cocktail.

We kept having crying spells. I would try to return to normal, but could not. At one point we were laughing and crying all at the same time, completely out of control. It took hours for the effects to wear off. But when they finally did we were left depressed, anxious, empty, sad and suicidal.

The only way to get rid of these negative feelings was to take more drugs. So I lived under the influence of those drug mixtures twenty-four hours a day. I worked at the swimming pool factory during the day, sniffed cocaine at work, went to school at night, and continued until three in the morning — using whatever drug appeared in front of me, mixing any combination of drugs available. But there was still one more thing that would drag me down even further.

CHAPTER V

As if this world of illusion that was eating away at my dignity were not enough, I allowed the worst, most devastating of all drugs to enter my life. Crack, the rock of death, appeared on the Brazilian drug scene between 1986 and 1987, and made its presence felt in São Paulo, the largest consumer market in the country.

The effects of crack are cruel and nonstop. In my case, I gave up almost every other drug for this yellow rock. Its rapid effect immediately drove me on. But when the effects wore off, the despair was crushing. I constantly wanted one more rock. It was maddening. It was scary. I had never seen anything like it. It gave me a sense of euphoria similar to cocaine, but it also gave me brief hallucinations. One of them was the feeling of being chased. I met people who would hear voices and see animals.

Crack became my companion during nights of prostitution. I slept with women who exchanged their bodies for a rock of crack or a line of cocaine. I snorted cocaine by the meter. I was the record holder among all my friends. Each line of cocaine was the width of a finger.

Crack

Crack cocaine is the crystal form of cocaine, which normally comes in a powder form. It comes in solid blocks or crystals varying in color from yellow to pale rose or white. Crack is heated and smoked. It is so named because it makes a cracking or popping sound when heated. Crack, the most potent form in which cocaine appears, is also the riskiest.

<u>SIDE EFFECTS:</u> loss of appetite, increased heart rate, muscle spasms and convulsions; severe depression, paranoia, dependence and suicidal tendencies.

ADAPTED FROM

This is a painful subject for me to speak about, since I was the one in my group of friends who smoked and sniffed the most. I got to the point of selling a motorcycle, and in one, single week spent every bit of that money on crack. I was a young man enslaved by my own urges. I obeyed the dictates of my senses. I had turned into a crackhead, the typical crack junkie. Any new experience was seductive to me.

Personal collection of the author

> *"We couldn't stop. We would binge
> on drugs for two or three days straight,
> until we couldn't handle anymore.
> I would say, 'No more. I don't want
> anymore,' but then something
> would pull us back down..."*
>
> **Lu F**

But I didn't do drugs in order to harm myself or anyone else. In my head, new experiences were good for me. Certain sensations were good at the time, but were only illusions. The pleasure I felt at the beginning was soon replaced by the bitterness of depression. All this led to an advanced phase of dependency.

I dedicated myself to crack like a conscientious student preparing for the entrance exams of death. It was common to stay up till the early morning hours without sleep, under the influence of drugs. I reached the point of smoking thirty to forty rocks in one night. I can safely say that the amount of drugs I consumed in four years, many have not consumed in twenty years.

And yet, nothing about my social life had changed. I enjoyed new friends, chasing little upper-middle-class girls and wore nice clothes. I wanted the complete package. Of course, this is not the reality for most addicts. In virtually all cases, crack drives people to abject poverty.

Time passed and I grew older in that fallen world. I turned 16, and then 17, and on both occasions I immersed myself in crack. But now that I was old enough, I would have to enter the military, which in the countryside of Brazil is called "Tiros de Guerra", a type of Army Reserve.

Tiros de Guerra

Military service is mandatory for men in Brazil. Some are allowed nine-month service terms but are expected to complete high school at the same time. These are called "Tiros de Guerra" or "shooting schools", which are for high school boys in medium-sized interior towns, run by Army senior NCO, Sergeant Majors or First Sergeants, rarely a Second Lieutenant.

ADAPTED FROM

While I was in the military I was lit up on drugs most of the time. I lived with men in the same situation as me, and I admit that I started to deal cocaine so that I could smoke crack and carry on with my sexual escapades. The truth is that I introduced lots of other guys to cocaine during my time in the service. Contrary to what most people think, drugs make their appearance at every level of society. There is no place that's free from them. There's a subtle language that connects all drug users. A gesture, a look, a key word. That's all it takes to establish communication. "Hey, you got powder?" That's all that's needed. A simple question communicates a vast amount of information between two people who've never seen each other before.

The problem of crack in Brazil is so severe, that São Paulo City Hall recently set up facilities in a downtown area called Crackland (Cracolândia). The project offers crack addicts jobs, housing, food and treatment, but no spiritual guidance.

We pass by addicts every single day without even realizing it. People who've just snorted cocaine or smoked weed move around normally in their jobs or neighborhoods. At 18 I completed my military service in which I had been high on drugs on a daily basis. At that time, I began to consume larger quantities of drugs, but never stopped using cocaine, which I bought in plastic bags. One particular time I bought a kilo of cocaine and the same amount of marijuana all at the same time.

Ziplock bags of cocaine

Ziplock bags are currently the most common containers for packaging drugs. Some can hold from five to twenty grams. Previously, cocaine was wrapped in aluminum foil or paper.

Fotolia

I would buy bags of cocaine that had between ten and twenty grams of the drug. I would sniff lines the length of a tabletop that were as wide as my finger. As a result, up till today I have nosebleeds. The mucous membrane of my nose is still very sensitive because of the abuse I put it through.

One thing that needs to be clarified is that young adults are not interested in explanations and lectures. Feelings are what count to them. Government lectures in school assemblies are for the most part worthless. Public money is being thrown away. Kids will always be kids.

The drug was in my life for seven years, which sounds like a short time. But the effects left deep scars. How am I still alive? I have no idea. My love of sports and daily exercise, especially during my time in the Army, might have something to do with it.

At this time in my life crack use became intense. I used a lot of cocaine when I was on duty, to keep me alert, and mixed it with all sorts of others drugs. When I had reached a saturation point, crack arrived with full force.

I never abandoned the other drugs, but crack became an obsession. I would do anything for it. I would sell anything for more crack. I had finally lost control. So I decided to leave the Army, the same way I had left university and my accounting degree – I gave up in the third semester.

I met addicts of every kind during this period of my life. Back then I never dreamed of having a good life, because I was already completely ruled by my addictions. I had very little hope that I would get out alive. Crack wielded so much power over me; its strength overwhelmed me. My personality was gone. I had no character, no dignity, no dreams and no hope.

CHAPTER VI

I realized that I was living on the edge, and so I made the radical decision to move to another city. I remembered that my uncle Luís, my father's brother, lived in Americana, a city in the state of São Paulo, the same state I was in. Imagining that distance would protect me from friends and from my own addictions, I packed my bags with all the confidence in the world.

I was putting an end to a troubled phase of my life and was making a change for the better. At least, that's what I wanted. I was no longer welcome in Lucélia. I'd developed a reputation, was a marked person, and that left me with few opportunities or options. But changing addresses does not force the spirit of addiction to stop its attacks. I was changing cities, but my life was still the same.

Would living in a new city be the answer or would I revert back to the same old escapes? Cutting off my Lucélia friends was a decision I made at the height of despair, thinking that it would save me from ruin. My uncle Luís was a businessman that had been through a lot in life and would be able to take care of me, to help me control my addiction. At least, that's what I thought.

It was also what I wanted. I didn't know how, but I wanted to get rid of my addiction. I didn't want to disappoint my parents, so I left Lucélia for a town where no one knew anything about me. It would be a new opportunity, a chance to start over. Living with my uncle was my chance to end this nightmare, a dream come true.

> *"I remember when Roger arrived in Americana. It was during Carnival and we drank a lot. But cigarettes and alcohol weren't enough for him, he wanted drugs. So I took him to the house of a friend and they started smoking crack together, inside a room. My friend's mother begged them to stop, but they refused. She cried and begged them to stop in God's name, but it was no use."*
>
> **Tatinho[3]**

But not all that glitters is gold. I should have paid attention to certain details of my uncle's life. Yes, he was a businessman, but he owned a bar, and ironically was a fall-down-drunk alcoholic. Without a doubt, this was not the ideal place for my recovery.

---

[3]Manoel Lança Junior, a friend in Americana.

*Luís Formigoni's bar,
my uncle in Americana.
From the personal
collection of the author.*

But the move had already been made, and I learned about his addiction too late. He gave me a room at the back of the bar. Before moving to the city I had sold a motorcycle and deposited the money in the bank. Right after I arrived and settled in, I met Adilson[4], who I called Dilsinho. He was a young man with a serious crack habit, and lived just opposite my uncle's bar. The very next day I was back on the rock of death.

> *"We would always use the bar of Big Rodge's
> uncle to get lit. We would lock the gate, turn
> the radio on real quiet like, smoke the stuff
> and then go out. It was always like that. We
> didn't go there too much because we didn't
> want to draw the attention of the neighbors."*
> **Dilsinho**

My life was stuck in addiction. I couldn't see any way out of my daily routine of drug use. The worst part was trying to get free while living in the home of an alcoholic with a crackhead

---

[4]Adilson Franciso Miguel da Silva, friend in Americana. His nickname was Dilsinho.

as my neighbor. Dilsinho was a well-known auto mechanic who worked on race cars. He earned good money, but sadly spent it all on his addiction. Like my friend Luciano, who spent a fortune on this degrading lifestyle, Adilson kept sinking further into crack, cocaine and marijuana.

> *"With crack, the more you smoke, the more you want to smoke. You're even willing to die for the stuff. You smoke and smoke, but are never satisfied. It's always like that. We would sell the sneakers off our feet, watches, shirts, car radios... I can't remember how many times Roger and I ripped out the radio from the dashboard and gave it to a dealer for one rock."*
>
> **Dilsinho**

There was no light at the end of the tunnel for me. After some time I was invited to a deliverance meeting of the Universal Church. Leonilda said that the Church had some really good rehab meetings; she was one of Dilsinho's sisters (we called her Ita[5]). Without quite understanding how, I realized that the Church really could do something about the mess I found myself in.

---

[5]Leonilda Miguel da Silva, the friend who first took Roger Formigoni to the Universal Church.

> *"One night, at three in the morning,*
> *we arrived at the Matiense favela [6] in a car*
> *that was extremely low on gas. We had no*
> *more money or drugs. We were on our way*
> *back from Capivari. We entered the favela.*
> *He had a beautiful wristwatch… I think*
> *it was a gift from his cousin. He traded*
> *the watch and the shirt he was*
> *wearing for three rocks."*
>
> *Dilsinho*

Although I had always heard a lot of people badmouthing the Universal Church, I decided to give in. Why resist one more invitation? How could my life get any worse? Soon afterwards I understood that the Church worked to save people like me, who were lost in the tangled maze of drugs.

> *"We used drugs together for a good while.*
> *I watched him lose a motorcycle, while I lost*
> *a car. Crack even took the sneakers off our*
> *feet. At one point we smoked forty rocks*
> *each in one night. He went to the bank*
> *machine to withdraw money nineteen*
> *separate times that night."*
>
> *Dilsinho*

---

[6] Very poor ghetto-like areas where people build makeshift homes and where violence, drugs and gangs abound.

I accepted the invitation to the Church as if it were an ordinary choice I made every day, like the hundreds of times I had allowed myself be taken down the path of some new drug. Though I was going to church, I was still using drugs, especially crack. In just one week I smoked all the money I had gotten from my motorcycle. All on crack. The next step was to start taking money from the cash register at the bar without uncle Luís finding out. But when he found out he balled me out and then told my parents. It became a huge family crisis. "What are we going to do about Roger?" My dad wanted to take me back to Lucélia where he could keep track of me, and help heal me.

> "The effects of the drugs made us want to get away from everyone. We went to all sorts of nasty, deserted places, just so we could smoke in peace."
> **Dilsinho**

The only people who did not turn their backs on me at that time were my parents. In tough times we can only count on a father, a mother and God. Every one of my friends and relatives kept their distance, saying there was no cure for my addiction. In reality my life had been reduced to smoking crack, having sex and sleep, which had robbed me of any hope for the future. But I now understood that it had not been worth it.

I told my dad that I would not return; it was unnecessary. I told him I was going to rehab meetings at a church. What they did not realize is that these meetings were in the Universal

Church… Before my uncle told my parents what kind of life I was living, my sister had been the only one in the family that knew the real state of my life. She would give me money; maybe she thought it would help protect me from the dangers that plague addicts. There were times she spent practically her entire salary on me.

> "An episode I'll never forget is when Big Rodge, Dui and I went to a crackhouse to get some rocks, but had no money to pay. I knew the dealer, so he gave us the drugs on condition that we'd pay the next day. When we went back the dealer suddenly started a fight with Big Rodge. Then the police showed up and searched everyone. They wanted to take us downtown, but somehow let us go."
>
> *Dilsinho*

Then I got into a fight with my uncle and had nowhere to go. That's when Gaúcho, Ita's husband, invited me to move in with them. They believed in my desire to get free; they felt I was genuine. As so I was able to get away from the problematic environment of the bar, and avoid returning to Lucélia to live with my parents. I started working in Gaúcho's maintenance and equipment repair company. From that moment on, I can say that the intensity of the storm began to show signs of dying out. But my situation was still complicated.

"I used crack cocaine and marijuana. I had given up pride, friends and possessions for drugs. Formigoni and I got to the point of smoking forty rocks in one night. We went to the dealer to get the drugs, and when we had finished, we went to an ATM to withdraw more money for more rocks. We went to that ATM nineteen different times that single night and used around one hundred rocks. One time he exchanged a watch and a shirt for three rocks. Another night we drove over six hundred kilometers by car smoking crack all the way. That day he had an overdose. We were on the road with two other friends, Rato and Dui. We had already smoked a lot. Suddenly Big Rodge began to have convulsions and started foaming at the mouth. We didn't know what to do. We stopped at a gas station, gave him some water, wet the back of his neck and then took him home. He refused to go to hospital for fear of the police. This is an addict's biggest fear."

Dilsinho

O v e r d o s e

An overdose is defined as the intentional or accidental ingestion of a drug over the normal or recommended amount. The body responds with severe symptoms because it is overwhelmed and is unable to metabolize the drug quickly enough. An overdose can cause a person to fall into unconsciousness, enter a state of psychosis or experience painful symptoms. Each type of overdose poses significant health risks, including contributing to a person's death. Illicit drugs have a higher risk of causing an overdose than prescription medication.

ADAPTED FROM

I was a young man of 19 whose life was in limbo. A short time ago, I had had no goals; my life was lost in the tangled maze of addictions, smoking forty rocks in one night.

This may be hard to understand for those not acquainted with the effect of this drug. You don't smoke an entire rock all at once. An addict breaks off pieces from a rock and smokes each piece separately. One rock of crack can mean up to seventy hits on a pipe.

In my case, this means that I reached the point of taking close to three thousand hits of crack in less than twenty-four hours. Almost anything can be used as a pipe. Even innocent-looking plastic cup can be adapted. I know all this because I spent years in the endless corridors of this maze.

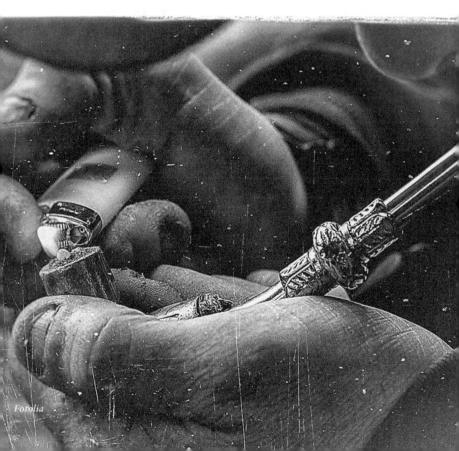

Fotolia

> *"Big Rodge didn't work, because he'd left Lucélia to get away from drugs. Sometimes he played at his uncle's bar, and then it was alcohol all day long. At night when we went out, he would do crack. It was like that. During the day it was alcohol; at night it was crack."*
>
> **Dilsinho**

When I decided to go to church, my uncle Luís came with me. He had made up with me without forcing me to move back to the bar. As I mentioned earlier, he was seriously addicted to the mother of all drugs, alcohol. Not everyone knows this, but alcohol is a stimulant and a depressive. My uncle drank to the extreme, maybe because he was the bar owner. He could not quit this addiction, or his addiction to tobacco, his other weakness.

A l c o h o l

Alcohol is a depressant, meaning that it slows down vital functions — resulting in slurred speech, unsteady movement, disturbed perceptions and an inability to react quickly. It reduces a person's ability to think rationally and distorts his or her judgment.

<u>SIDE EFFECTS:</u> acts negatively on metabolism, cause euphoria, loss of social inhibitions, expansive behavior, and exaggerated emotion; in some cases, explosively belligerent or aggressive behavior.

ADAPTED FROM

When my uncle drank, he changed. It seemed like there was another person inside of him. He was also lost in the tangled maze of drugs. But when the effects wore off, he would not remember anything that had happened. He went with me to church, heard the same messages that I heard, the same encouraging words, but chose not to run with it.

Fotolia

My uncle committed suicide some time later, by hanging. When it happened, I had already broken free from the world of drugs and was a pastor. My uncle witnessed all the changes in my life, but did not have the strength to let go and allow himself to be saved. He was the youngest in my father's family. He ended his life before the age of 40, a victim of the depression that alcohol brings.

Because uncle Luís did not know how to get rid of his pain, he destroyed one of the greatest gifts bestowed to man: life. He would not allow himself to be saved. In my case, I was saved through an invitation to the Universal Church, and through my refusal to give up.

> *"In one month, I saw Roger and my brother Dilsinho spend two thousand reais (Brazilian currency) on crack. Roger was skin and bones, was pale and had dark circles around his eyes. On the rare occasion that he ate lunch, he would not eat dinner. He was on the edge. No one took an interest in him. But one evening, as I was getting ready to go to church, he came to the door and asked where I was going. When I told him, he asked if I would invite him along."*
>
> *Ita*

We need to understand that not everyone can change their mindset when invitations are made. Dilsinho, my "partner in crime," was given the same invitation that I was given, but didn't take advantage of it at the time, just like my uncle. Fortunately we can count on Dilsinho's testimony for this book because he is now a restored man.

Now let's talk about how I came to be saved.

> "Faith makes all the difference. In Roger's case, his only hope was Jesus. His uncle treated him very badly, and at one point even forced Roger to choose between living in his house and attending the Universal Church. I helped save his soul from that filthy, rotten life with the help of my husband. One day when my car broke down, my husband helped me take Roger to church. When we noticed a change in him, my husband said that Roger should come and stay in our home."
>
> **Ita**

CHAPTER VII

It's not enough to simply hear the message when you choose to be saved from the misery of addiction. You need to accept that message of truth. The salvation of a person who is in the situation that I was in cannot happen at the snap of a finger. "But what happened to you? How did you get free?"

When people ask me this, I always tell them: You have nothing more to lose when you've become an addict — drugs have taken everything you had. At that point of my life, I was unconsciously following an impressive example of faith from the Bible that made me rethink every step I took on that path from hell. It's the story of the Syrian General, Naaman, who was blessed by the Lord through the prophet Elisha.

> "Naaman was general of the army under the king of Aram. He was important to his master, who held him in the highest esteem because it was by him that God had given victory to Aram: a truly great man, but afflicted with a grievous skin disease. It so happened that Aram, on one of its raiding expeditions against Israel, captured a young

girl who became a maid to Naaman's wife. One day she said to her mistress, 'Oh, if only my master could meet the prophet of Samaria, he would be healed of his skin disease.' Naaman went straight to his master and reported what the girl from Israel had said. 'Well then, go,' said the king of Aram. 'And I'll send a letter of introduction to the king of Israel.' So he went off, taking with him about 750 pounds of silver, 150 pounds of gold, and ten sets of clothes. Naaman delivered the letter to the king of Israel. The letter read, 'When you get this letter, you'll know that I've personally sent my servant Naaman to you; heal him of his skin disease.' When the king of Israel read the letter, he was terribly upset, ripping his robe to pieces. He said, 'Am I a god with the power to bring death or life that I get orders to heal this man from his disease? What's going on here? That king's trying to pick a fight, that's what!' Elisha the man of God heard what had happened, that the king of Israel was so distressed that he'd ripped his robe to shreds. He sent word to the king, 'Why are you so upset, ripping your robe like this? Send him to me so he'll learn that there's a prophet in Israel.' So Naaman with his horses and chariots arrived in style and stopped at Elisha's

> door. Elisha sent out a servant to meet him
> with this message: 'Go to the River Jordan
> and immerse yourself seven times. Your
> skin will be healed and you'll be as good as
> new.' Naaman lost his temper. He turned
> on his heel saying, 'I thought he'd personal-
> ly come out and meet me, call on the name
> of God, wave his hand over the diseased
> spot, and get rid of the disease. The Damas-
> cus rivers, Abana and Pharpar, are cleaner
> by far than any of the rivers in Israel. Why
> not bathe in them? I'd at least get clean.'
> He stomped off, mad as a hornet. But his
> servants caught up with him and said,
> 'Father, if the prophet had asked you to
> do something hard and heroic, wouldn't
> you have done it? So why not this simple
> "wash and be clean"?' So he did it. He
> went down and immersed himself in the
> Jordan seven times, following the orders of
> the Holy Man. His skin was healed; it was
> like the skin of a little baby. He was as
> good as new."
>
> **2 Kings 5:1-14 (MSG)**

General Naaman could never have imagined that his healing would come from the River Jordan. It doesn't make sense for a dirty river to be the source of healing for a sick person. And yet, just like Naaman was healed of his leprosy by immersing himself in the Jordan, I found permanent healing from the addictions that troubled and destroyed me in the Universal Church.

The Jordan River was not clean like the Abana and Pharpar rivers in Damascus. If other people had done what Naaman was told to do, its waters would have absorbed sicknesses of people on an immense scale. The Universal Church is similar in that it is a church that welcomes all who are, in some way, living a substandard life, abandoned in the maze of addictions, and in need of help. Just as the healing of Naaman occurred in the Jordan, my healing occurred in the Universal Church.

Its name is associated with impurity, but healing takes place within its premises. It happens to be this way because it needs to offer shelter to those in need of help, even if they are social "lepers" who inhabit the lower end of what this world values. The Universal Church accepts all people without distinction, for the purpose of freeing them from everything that contaminates and destroys their lives.

I'm not saying that God loves sin — I am saying He loves the sinner. It would be a great cruelty if people who acknowledged their mistakes and were genuinely repentant were forever abandoned in this world because of a foolish mistake. If God forgave David's betrayal at the cost of his firstborn, and forgave the brutality of Saul of Tarsus and allowed him to be reborn as the apostle Paul, why would He not forgive anyone else who truly wants to be saved?

> *"All that the Father gives Me will come to Me, and the one who comes to Me I will by no means cast out."*
> *John 6:37 (NKJV)*

Rich or poor, healthy or sick, whether their problem is in their body or in their mind, we need to be accepting of those who are rejected by their families or by society, and offer them healing. In the case of Naaman, we know that he wanted to know why he could not immerse himself in other cleaner rivers. But Elisha the prophet saw the Jordan as a suitable environment for the general's healing precisely because he felt revulsion for it.

It was no different for me. "You could have gone to any church. Why did you have to go there?" was what people kept

telling me, especially my family. My answer could not have been more of a contrast: "I'm seeking God, don't you see? When I was on drugs, you complained; now that I'm going to church, you're still complaining!"

When I first entered the Church this is what I learned. The spirit of addiction that had been tormenting me for years knew that my healing and deliverance were in that place, and that both would come from the Lord Jesus. And so it fought back and tried to make me give up. But I was determined and refused to consider retreat.

I started going to meetings every day of the week. It was not difficult to go to church every day, just like I had not found it difficult to use drugs every day. At a certain point I decided to use all the strength I had to take hold of the miracle that I was looking for. There was only one way to know whether or not the pastor's preaching was true — I would have to put everything he said into practice.

Suddenly, a conviction I never imagined I could have rose up inside of me: "If no obstacle was ever considered too difficult when I was looking to score drugs, why would I not have the same attitude in surrendering to God?" And so, I held on to the habit of going to church every day and I began to understand and identify what was behind my addiction. Everything had been caused by an evil spirit — the spirit of addiction.

Attending meetings every day was the only way to control the spirit that I now knew had made me obsessed with drugs. I avoided contact with my old drug buddies, and most importantly, Dilsinho, my addict-neighbor. I went to church every night. I didn't follow the traditional weekly meeting routine suggested by the Church (2 or 3 times a week). I would go to meetings every day, and would put into practice everything that I heard the pastor say. I felt I needed to absorb everything.

That began to help me, and people started asking me how I was doing it. I can only say that it was a process of surrendering to God. Pure and simple surrender. After a little more than a month of going back and forth to meetings, mistakes and failures started to become obvious to me, as well as my serious lack of intelligence in making decisions... So I decided to surender.

The truth is, it was very easy to surrender to God. Like any addict, I had a real knack for surrender because I had done it every day when I released my grasp on my dignity and surrendered to drugs. Why not surrender to God? That day it all began to make sense and I had an encounter with God, I experienced Him, and I was forever changed on the inside.

That was a Sunday. I remember as if it were today. It seemed like I was all alone in the meeting, even though it was packed. Everything that came out of the pastor's mouth was a word of God directed to me. That day I came to my senses, my mistakes and sins became abundantly clear to me, and I decided to surrender myself to God, body, soul and spirit.

The day I made this choice, I said to God: "From today on, I will never disappoint You again!" At that moment I yielded in humility

In a meeting during my healing process. Personal collection of the author

to the Lord with all that I was. I felt and received a satisfaction in my soul that I had never experienced before. Strength and courage rained down on me with an intensity that far, far surpassed anything that drugs had given me in those lost years of my life.

My encounter with God was complete. At that moment I was coming into contact with something I had never experienced before. At that moment a radical transformation took place in my mind. I made a prayer and promised Him that crack, marijuana, cocaine and the rest would never rule over me ever again, and I intended to prove the truth of what I had promised.

I began to have a strength that I had never possessed in my life, and to experience a level of self-control that I had never had. In spite of this, in the mind of my family (who would soon discover my new state of being) I was still an addict and was still using drugs even though I was going to church. No one believed that I had managed to free myself from my addiction. But the fact was that I had been reshaped that day. I was stronger… so much so that when I got home after the meeting, Dilsinho came looking for me. He offered me a bag of crack for free. There must have been about thirty rocks in that bag.

"This bag's for you. You don't owe me anything. It's to make up for all the times you shared your stuff with me." I looked straight into his eyes and said, "Thanks, but I don't want it. I found God today, and He's much more powerful than any rock." My recovery began right there, and at the same time, a challenge.

A voice echoed in my mind twenty-four hours a day, telling me to smoke one last rock and then stop. That voice tormented me for three days nonstop, repeating that message of defeat. "Smoke the last rock, then you can stop." I even had insomnia and chills, but I won.

CHAPTER VIII

Quitting my addictions was an enormous challenge. In my period of drug use I lived in a world full of feelings and stimulants, but empty of spirituality. I could do anything. I felt powerful. I was sure that society's rules did not apply to me. But even so, none of it could compare to the happiness I experienced the day I surrendered to God. Something had changed inside me and I was able to resist the voice that kept insisting that I smoke the last rock.

Every person that's freed from an addiction will continue to live with a voice like the one that tormented me for a long time. This is a manifestation of the voice of the spirit of addiction that knows (in its mind) that it cannot lose the addict. In my case, it was three days of agony. The only way through was to resist it with all my might and ask God for help.

I promised never to disappoint Jesus again, so I resisted all the attacks of that voice. The voice caused deep depression, anxiety and pressure. It was a fight that I was waging against the spirit of addiction who was trying for the last time to reconquer me. On the third day it was as if I had never smoked a day in my life. The urges, the desire, vanished; I was now disgusted with drugs.

> *"Therefore submit to God. Resist the devil*
> *and he will flee from you."*
>
> **James 4:7 (NKJV)**

Though I did not know the Bible at the time, I was able to resist. On that third day, the spirit had left. From that moment on, the change that had begun when I truly surrendered to Jesus was complete. The urge to get all drugged up was gone, but I still wasn't out of the woods.

From that day on, my life took off. I continued to go to church every day, wanting to learn more about spiritual things. After a while, Gaúcho invited me to be his partner in a business venture. He wanted to set up a factory to produce fiberglass motorcycle helmets and customized spare parts for various applications.

He knew about my experience with fiberglass swimming pools, and the fact that I had mastered that skill fit perfectly with his new idea. Since Ayrton Senna was at his peak of popularity at the time, the company's specialty was helmets, and in particular, competition helmets. We also produced fiberglass add-ons for cars and trucks.

I had truly been reshaped as a man. At that moment I was returning to where it all began — working once again with the hydrocarbons that had ruined my adolescence. Can you guess what happened? Absolutely nothing. To tell you the truth, I had to start using a mask because the smell of those chemicals, especially thinner, made me feel physically sick.

Working at Gaúcho's company (Ita's husband). Personal collection of the author.

This was the beginning of my new life. For this new journey, I rented a room and lived alone. After some time, we shut the business down and I found an office job. I was another person! I rented a house and continued to build up my life. By that time I had already had my encounter with God and had been born of God. I had been baptized in water, had received the confirmation of the Holy Spirit and had already been raised as an assistant, a person dedicated to serving God on the altar.

> *"An assistant makes him/herself available to suffering people. They make an effort to take the Word of God to needy people in hospitals, prisons, nursing homes or wherever they may be found."*
> **Bishop Sergio Corrêa**

I continued to work as an assistant (prayer counselor) but was facing down an immense challenge: To show the people around me that faith had the power to shield a person from the spiritual death of addictions. I knew I was contradicting the psychological principle that says that addiction is a complex disease. They claim that former addicts almost always relapse when they come in contact with the substance to which they used to be addicted. I am living proof that this is not an absolute truth.

Current medical thinking defines drug addiction as a disease just like any other physical ailment. It has a biological basis, characteristic signs and symptoms, a sequence, predictable results and disclaims "international" causation... The wide variety of existing definitions and modes of treatment of chemical dependencies reveals that there is no single characterization which is able to sufficiently describe or explain addiction. It should be regarded as a progressive, incurable, potentially fatal, multifaceted disease, affecting human beings in all areas of their life: physical, mental and social.

ADAPTED FROM

Fotolia

I decided to be more radical and test myself in bigger ways. At one point I went back to Lucélia and met up with my old friends. They still had the same old habits, mostly cocaine. I told them about Jesus and about my recovery, in the hope that they would respond.

All they wanted to know was if I still sniffed. There they were, in front of me, using cocaine and offering it to me, as always. So I told them firmly: "If you keep offering me this powder, I'll blow it all away and then you'll be left with nothing!" Then they truly realized that I had changed.

After that, and in many other situations, it became clear that the change that Jesus had performed in me was tougher by far than any manifestation of the spirit of addiction in people who crossed my path. For example, drug dealers who I used to buy drugs from kept on contacting me, offering drugs, but to no effect.

People who were used to seeing me smoking and drinking all day long, noticed the change and would say, "Wow! He's sober. He's not high on drugs anymore…" And they would start guessing as to why. But the quick response would come: "What got him off drugs was Jesus, through the Universal Church."

Of course many were suspicious, making jokes about how it could never last, labeling my healing a flash in the pan. But users from my old circle of friends, and dealers from the neighborhood and their customers, made a point of searching me out and asking if it was true that I didn't want anything, had I really and truly stopped.

The answer was always the same: "I'm going to church. I don't use any of that anymore." Even so, they offered me drugs for free and I always refused. This became a routine during my period of deliverance… my treatment. Offers were constant, and my job was to refuse them, to never give in.

I was totally determined. I had made a promise to God, and no matter what, I was going to keep it down to the letter. I was not going to disappoint God. I kept my word and resisted. The strength I received at the moment of my surrender to Jesus, and not a second before, is at the heart of my message to people who contact me in my day-to-day work.

This is also true for those who do not want drug addictions to enter their homes. Learning the ins and outs of protecting yourself and your family from addictions is something that concerns everyone. Everyone wants to avoid the presence of drugs in their homes.

And yet, many people only do something about this problem or ask for help after they've experienced it firsthand. Drugs have to invade their homes before they open their eyes. My mother is an example of this. She only realized that I was a drug addict after I had already sunk deep into crack. Most families discover that their loved one is an addict only two or three years after the addiction has begun.

And so, no matter how much we spread the message about the danger of addiction, many assume it will never happen to them. People don't understand the mechanism of how drugs manipulate people into turning their backs on the things and people that they love. A silent process that drives you to throw away your money, your friends, your family, your home, your dignity…

Drugs destroy society. When an addiction invades a home, love goes out the window. On top of this, misinformation is a weapon that allows the spirit of addiction to go unnoticed. Drugs destroy us from the inside out. They eat away at our bodies, and mark our souls for extermination.

CHAPTER IX

When I think of everything I left behind, my many failures and the routine of senseless behavior involving people who were unable get out of the quicksand of addiction that was swallowing them, I consider myself privileged. I found a way back from a journey that could easily have been a one-way trip. The spirit of addiction has a ravenous appetite and does not forgive the bodies it takes possession of. It makes a person plunge into and drown in the sea of drugs, destroying him without mercy. I've seen this many times when evil manifested in people.

But with faith we can overpower this spirit of addiction and rebuild our lives. The faith to do this comes from the Word of God. This faith enables your body to overpower the cursed urge to take drugs. Faith is life, and you are a child of God destined to live in the abundance and health of a drug-free life.

Today, I help people get rid of their addictions by introducing them to Jesus. In my day-to-day work, I meet people who are suffering because of the evil that addictions are creating in them, or in their loved ones. I see every sort of destruction you can imagine in the meetings that we make in the Universal Church for people suffering with addictions.

In one of these meetings I saw a demon. This spirit was manifesting in front of the pastor, who was asking him questions — the spirit of addiction in action. He said that he put disease in the possessed person's body. "I make her fight, I give her disease, I give her addictions... I get high through her, I drink through her, I snort through her." That's when I understood what had been happening to me all those years. When I heard that demon, I realized that I had been a channel to satisfy a demon, the spirit of addiction. He had been sniffing, smoking and doing drugs through my body! He had been controlling me, and I had been slowly dying because of those addictions.

> "We had no future. All we had were
> flipflops, shorts and t-shirts. We would say,
> 'If we don't do something, we're gonna die.'
> After fourteen hours straight of crack
> cocaine — and all sweaty — we didn't even
> know what to say. It was really hard."
> **Dilsinho**

I have to say that in most cases this spirit does not manifest. It works in the mind, manipulating a person's will. This is how the spirit of addiction controls an addict.

A victim is willing to sacrifice family, children, job and dreams for a substance. Where's the person's awareness of what's going on? The spirit destroys it; he transforms the addict into his own slave.

When an addict is possessed, parents leave their children, and husbands leave their wives and are not in the least worried about whether or not their family will have enough to eat. The addiction becomes the number one priority of the addict, because he is being ruled over. He is lucid for a few moments, knows that his addiction is destroying his life, but has no power to get out of it, no control over himself. A voice echoes in his head, saying: "Only do it today, only this once. Only today." Meanwhile, he sinks deeper and deeper in debt.

I welcome people into our church who are totally destroyed. Once there was a guy who had been in recovery for twelve weeks. He had nosedived into the "delights" of crack and had paid a very high price. This businessman lost his family, his marriage of thirteen years, all his earthly possessions — including stores and restaurants — his home, dignity, self-respect and finally, his honor. For a period of seventeen years, marijuana, alcohol, cocaine and finally crack took everything he had built up.

He ended up on the street. This man who had once earned $60,000 a month, was dragged down to the very lowest level of society to live in Crackland (São Paulo). He got to the point of trading the clothes he was wearing for a very small rock of crack. And he told me what I already knew: This is the unavoidable fate of anyone who uses crack. Then I told him (twelve weeks ago) what he needed to know, that Jesus is stronger than crack. If the tangled maze of addictions exists, this man is proof that He is the only way out.

But most people see no hope or possibility of ever getting out of this maze. People go to clinics, see psychologists, seek all kinds of help, but cannot find anything to transform their wrecked lives. This man could not find help even in the church he used to attend — "That's not the place for me. I'm hopeless." Then one day he saw the TV program The Last Rock and said, "Wow! Now that's for me. That's my problem."

"This new path caught my attention.
It was a critical time for me...
living in my father's house and being
supported by him... fighting with
my ex-wife and son. This was the state
I was in when I saw your program.
I wondered, would this work for me?
The simple act of watching
the program helped me to stay away
from cigarettes and other drugs."

After attending the meetings he became aware of his real problem and was able to get rid of his addiction spirit. But not everyone chooses this path.

Dealing with an addiction is a job that's always postponed, always left for later. The victim ceases to consume, and is himself consumed by the addiction, which traps and imprisons him. Then the truth — the real goal of the spirit of addiction — is revealed: Its job is to destroy its host, whom it infests like a virus.

There are no addicts that say they're happy, that have positive lives or that are able to achieve many dreams. All, without exception, are destroyed. Peace, harmony in the home, restful sleep? These do not exist in the world of an addict. I've never heard any addict testify that cocaine had improved his life. What we see on a daily basis in our services and on the program "The Last Rock" are terrifying stories of mothers who are afraid of losing their children, and children who attack their mothers by putting knives to their necks and saying:

"If you don't give me the money, I'll kill you."

Once, a wife came to talk to me and said that her husband had promised to stop using cocaine. But as soon as he was paid, he disappeared, and hadn't yet returned home. Without a doubt he had spent the money once again. She did not even have a pack of rice at home. She had to ask her mother-in-law for food in order to feed her children.

We help people who are considered incurable, as well as those who no longer believe that traditional scientific methods can cure them. According to drug rehab clinics, addiction is an incurable, progressive, fatal disease. One father of a cocaine addict claimed to have spent over 200,000 Brazilian Reals on medical treatments without success. But when he heard that addiction was a spirit, he realized that that was the answer to his son's problem with cocaine.

The fight to cure addictions challenges what science says is possible. I do not presume to question the effectiveness of science in any manner whatsoever, but I do want to show that addictions can be cured by presenting evidence of real-life cases like mine and others who were able to get rid of severe dependencies on drugs. There are many, many testimonies.

The method is extremely simple. All we have to do is remove the spirit of addiction from the person with drug dependence. The case of one man who came to me is a classic example. He had been addicted to cachaça (a strong Brazilian liquor) for forty-two years. He would drink around thirty shots during the day and a one-liter bottle every night. This man was fifty years old when he quit his addiction in 2014. An addiction he had developed as a boy.

He suffered from panic attacks. Every morning, he needed a shot, because of the hours during the night that he had gone without a drink. He couldn't do anything without a drink — he needed a shot before he left the house, He needed a shot before he talked to someone... He came to the Church and that same day, as soon as he left the meeting, he went to get a shot of cachaça.

"As soon as he swallowed the drink, he threw up and began to feel disgust for it."

Since then, not even a drop of cachaça has touched his mouth. What happened to him? It's simple. The spirit of addiction was removed from his body. The depression, irritation and anguish that had been destroying him... all of that left. There are many testimonies like this man's.

The same thing happened to a younger man with a similar story to the alcoholic's, who had a seventeen-year cocaine habit. He came to the first meeting with nothing, having moved in with a friend because he had no place to live. After ten weeks, all attempts to have any sort of contact with the drug would make him sick. In his own words...

"The strange thing is, the desire vanished."

He had gone to various rehabs, where he had been in lock-down for months in total abstinence — but his desire for drugs never left him. As soon as he would leave the rehab, he would start using again. But when he arrived at the Universal Church, the desire disappeared. He is one of many that have been healed through the treatments we perform.

I can also cite the case of a man who sold the family car for rocks of crack cocaine. Rocks that lasted a few days, like a puff of wind. But I did the same thing when I sold a motorcycle to buy the same drug. When these types of people look at possessions and money they only see rocks of crack. I know that.

And what is even more maddening is that an addict (user, junkie, druggie) accepts a dealer's "exchange rate." Simply put, if a dealer says that the microwave of an addict's mother is only worth two rocks, the poor guy will get the appliance and hand it over to the cheat without the blink of an eye.

These people quickly lose control, like the son who sold his mother's car for $20 worth of crack. (Read this report for yourself at http://zh.clicrbs.com.br/, published on 07/28/2010). What have we become? What goes on in the mind of a crackhead? Only God knows. And only He is able to provide the needed deliverance.

There are many, many examples of people who've gone off the deep end because of this demonic spirit. If I were to talk about all the sad cases I've come across, his book would never end. But I can also affirm, with immense satisfaction, that I would need a much larger book, or an infinite number of books to talk about the lives of the many people who are now healed of their addictions through faith in Jesus.

We have kept track of their progress, because it takes time for a person to rebuild their dignity. We do spiritual follow-up, and have noticed that the more people give themselves to God, the more faith they have, the more spiritual they become. I am one of them.

CHAPTER X

After all I went through, the question is, how is my life today? I am one of those people from the previous chapter, a purified Roger. I entered the Work of God after I had gone through my own process of healing and recovery. After working as an assistant pastor in Campinas, I was consecrated as a pastor and went to Itapira, in the São Paulo countryside, on the border with Minas Gerais (another state in Brazil). There I was given the responsibility to care for my first church. After working in Cosmópolis and Paulínia, I moved to the capital.

In São Paulo, I was the main pastor in the churches of Santana, Pinheiros, São Caetano, the old Brás, Lapa, Freguesia do Ó and João Dias. Then I was put in charge of the Financial Success meetings for the state of Minas Gerais and later led the work in the state of Ceará. The year that this book was first published in Brazil, 2014, I was consecrated a bishop. Now I dedicate myself, body and soul, to helping those who want to forever break free from addictions — like me, some years back. This is the mission of everyone who has been reborn in Jesus:

> *"Go into all the world and preach*
> *the gospel to every creature."*
> **Mark 16:15 (NET)**

Because of this, the Universal Church around the world is mobilizing to combat drug addiction, and I actively participate in this work by giving my testimony and helping in any way I can. I have been working to spread the news about these meetings of deliverance by showing the results of our work on the radio program "The Last Rock" (in Brazil) and daily spots on TV Record (Brazil).

But, as you can see in the preceding pages, before getting to this point — healed by Jesus, the true Rock — I stumbled a lot, and because of all that I had gone through, I never really believed that I would have my own family. Happily, I was wrong. I met my wife, Ana Claudia, in church. At least, I thought that was the first time we met, but we had already met without realizing it. Though I was officially introduced to her in Americana, her family had lived in Lucélia when Ana was a girl. Believe it or not, her family had lived a block away from my house, on the street above.

Years later, we "discovered" each other in Americana, a city almost five hundred kilometers away from Lucélia. Only after we met in church did we learn that our families had been neighbors and that they had even known each other. We dated for eleven months and then got married, and after six months of marriage we entered the Work of God and I became an assistant pastor. I've been married to Ana Claudia since 1997, completely drug-free and full of the Holy Spirit.

*Bishop Roger Formigoni and his wife,
Ana Claudia. A solid marriage since 1997.*

This abundance can only be found when we surrender to Jesus, the Rock, the Cornerstone of our faith, and are at last free from every chain that bound us to addictions.

> *"Jesus said to them, 'Have you never read in the Scriptures: "The stone which the builders rejected has become the chief cornerstone. This was the Lord's doing, and it is marvelous in our eyes"?'"*
> **Matthew 21:42 (NKJV)**

When I was finally introduced to Jesus — the Last Rock, the Cornerstone — on the day I was delivered, it produced in me a much more intense and powerful effect than anything I had ever experienced from drugs throughout my miserable, old life.

> *"Therefore, brothers, by the mercies of God, I urge you to present your bodies as a living sacrifice, holy and pleasing to God; this is your spiritual worship. Do not be conformed to this age, but be transformed by the renewing of your mind, so that you may discern what is the good, pleasing, and perfect will of God."*
> **Romans 12:1,2 (HCSB)**

The radical transformation that happened in me — and which happens to everyone that conquers the spirit of addition — created a new path in front of me and opened the gates to a renewed life. When my neighbor offered me that bag of crack and I immediately refused, immoveable in my determination to never use drugs again, I realized that the power of God — that was now taking care of me — had empowered me to crush the power of the spirit of addiction that was possessing "my friend."

Tasting the mighty power of the Lord was like experiencing an infinitely superior high much stronger than crack or any other type of drug. The time had come to allow the power of God to be manifested in me, and from then on I had the strength to be immoveable about my promise to the Lord Jesus: "I'll never disappoint You again!"

> *"Coming to Him, a living stone — rejected by men but chosen and valuable to God — you yourselves, as living stones, are being built into a spiritual house for a holy priesthood to offer spiritual sacrifices acceptable to God through Jesus Christ."*
> **1 Peter 2:4,5**

The strong, close relationship that I've come to have with the Lord Jesus Christ has helped me to understand that He is the Rock (Stone) of my life, an invaluable part of the Work of God. Unlike those who've chosen the wrong path to build their lives (Psalm 118:22), I chose to base my new life on the Living Stone, the First and the Last Rock, because He is the true foundation for man's eternal life (1 Corinthians 3:11).

The Universal Church is built on Jesus, the Cornerstone, and is made up of all people, all who need help, who decide to be reborn and who are prepared to follow the right path:

> *"So then you are no longer foreigners and strangers, but fellow citizens with the saints, and members of God's household, built on the foundation of the apostles and prophets, with Christ Jesus Himself as the cornerstone. The whole building, being put together by Him, grows into a holy sanctuary in the Lord. You also are being built together for God's dwelling in the Spirit."*
> **Ephesians 2:19-22 (HCSB)**

We need to base our lives on the eternal Rock (Stone). We need to lay our lives on it in order to receive the eternal support that we need. In the spiritual building of God, we declare the goodness of Him who called us out of darkness and into His marvelous light (1 Peter 2:7-9).

I overcame my fight against the flesh. I conquered the urge to get high and overcame the spirit of addiction. I resisted that cursed last rock. Under the protection of Jesus, I appeared to have never used drugs in my life. I was FREE! The urge to use drugs simply vanished. But today I realize that if I had not resisted that last rock of crack cocaine, you who are reading this book right now would not have a book to read.

The key to my deliverance was holding on to faith and to obedience to God, seeking Him every single day and allowing myself to be baptized in water... to be reborn into a renewed life. This is how I stayed faithful to the Lord. Once I had surrendered to Him, I didn't want to waste any more time.

Whoever wants to follow my path has to be faithful to God and rigorously attend meetings at the Universal Church, no matter what struggles, persecutions, difficulties or prejudices they face — even if it's a pure and simple lack of money for transport. If that's your case, then walk, but always believe. It'll be good for your health, especially your spiritual health.

All of us who decide to surrender our lives to Jesus will go through trying times; you will have to sidestep huge and fierce temptations. In the world of drugs there will always be an abundance of resources; as you know only too well, it's an "easy" life. But for those of us who seek God, the path of faith that we choose is much more difficult, especially when we're coming from the world of drugs. There were days I had no food to eat. But a power inside of me kept telling me that I would overcome that hard time. Though he was defeated, the voice of the spirit of addiction would appear out of the blue and argue that when I used drugs I had money, and now that I was serving God I was hungry...

> *"I have told you these things so that in Me you may have peace. You will have suffering in this world. Be courageous! I have conquered the world."*
> **John 16:33 (HCSB)**

But the power of God always wins out when we have faith. It speaks louder and sounds stronger. It is constantly telling us that we're going to overcome this world. Like me, you should take a firm hold of your faith, and gradually you will begin to see all of God's promises coming true in your day-to-day life. After that, a time will come when you experience an "overdose" of the Holy Spirit. You will feel His magnificent presence and hear His fantastic voice. As happened with me, the day that you are baptized in the Holy Spirit will be an extraordinary, unforgettable experience!

When we are reborn in Jesus, we become the owners of a conviction and power that we have never known. I immediately knew that God Himself now lived inside of me, that He was inhabiting my body, flowing through my veins and arteries, dwelling in my organs and respiratory system twenty -four hours a day!

> *"But you will receive power when the Holy Spirit has come on you, and you will be My witnesses in Jerusalem, in all Judea and Samaria, and to the ends of the earth."*
> **Acts 1:8 (HCSB)**

Drugs may give us a sense of euphoria, but their effect is only temporary. They never give us a permanent sense of fullness and abundance. On the other hand, when God and His Word come to occupy our body and mind 24/7, 365 days a year, the effect is so overwhelming that we never want Him to leave.

The effect of God's Word and the Holy Spirit in my body is magnificent. Because of this, I do all I can to communicate what happened to me in the best possible way in the hope that others may experience it too. And that includes those of you who are reading this testimony right now. I'm certain that you have gone through some type of experience in this world that brought you depression, loss, failure, defeat or loneliness.

Why not take advantage of this moment and surrender to God — the same life that no one else seems to value. I'm speaking about your life... a life that God will return to you completely transformed. Don't forget. Before Naaman could be healed, he had to immerse himself in the Jordan, a river that everyone looked down on, that was considered unclean and polluted. But that river was what cleansed Naaman.

The source of the healing for addictions, whatever your addiction may be, lies in simply immersing yourself — body and spirit —in the arms of the Lord Jesus. At the Universal Church, a place that's despised by many, like the Jordan in the time of Elisha, you will be purified of your addiction. I am sure that in a short period of time, you will be delivered and will be one of our next testimonies!

May God bless you!

Roger Formigoni, Bishop of the Universal Church

Whatever your addiction, psychiatry and professional rehabs claim that it is an incurable, progressive and potentially fatal disease, and that a chemically dependent person, or addict, will never enjoy a normal social life.

This book suggests the opposite.

THERE IS A CURE FOR ADDICTIONS!

No matter what you're addicted to, all you need to do is find the Last Rock. I'm not referring to religion, that you may already have. The Last Rock is the Lord Jesus. When you find Him, the healing of all your addictions will occur.

If you want to talk to me, please don't hesitate to contact me. I invite you to the Addiction Cleansing Therapy sessions every Sunday at Avenida João Dias, 1.800 — Santo Amaro, São Paulo, Brazil.

I am also on social networks, in particular Facebook. Here are my contacts:

 rogerioformigoni@r7.com

 www.facebook.com/BpFormigoni